Published by Frederick A. Praeger, Inc., New York

THE MAGIC

OF THE

OPERA

A Picture Memoir of the Metropolitan

WITH A SERIES
OF CONTEMPORARY
PHOTOGRAPHS BY
GJON MILI

TEXT BY
MARY ELLIS PELTZ

DESIGN BY
TINA S. FREDERICKS

in cooperation with the Metropolitan Opera Association

BOOKS THAT MATTER

Published in the United States of America in 1960
by Frederick A. Praeger, Inc., Publishers
64 University Place, New York 3, N. Y.
Copyright 1960 by the Metropolitan Opera Association
under the provisions of the International Copyright Union
All rights reserved
Library of Congress catalog card number 60-9011
Printed in Germany

Contents

A New

House for Opera

For nearly a century, the history of grand opera in America has been written in the Metropolitan Opera House. It is a history of music and drama, of glamor and scandal, of catastrophes and conflicts, of tragedies—and of triumphs. Coming to New York from Europe, grand opera brought with it those traditions of festive court life which, in the popular mind, held sway long before elegant ladies of the 1800's arrived in their carriages at the old Academy of Music (*above*). Today, as in the past, the tradition of jewels and flowers, of tiaras and top hats still shines in the opera house. So does the tradition of the great, curving horseshoe, from whose center box it was the custom of European monarchs to preside over the court. In the long history of the Metropolitan, however, other old traditions of opera have yielded to the new.

In 1883, New York had outgrown the old Academy of Music and reached uptown for a more commodious theater, the Metropolitan Opera House. Though the "early Italian Renaissance façade" of this new building was at first likened to a yellow brewery, the public admired its ivory and gold auditorium. Here was indeed a proper setting for grand opera, and, in this "veritable jewel box," gilded society applauded its favorite stars.

The first opera to be presented in the new house was *Faust*. Italian opera had set its stamp on America, and thus, despite its German origin and its French libretto, *Faust* was sung in the Italian language. Soon, however, Italian opera was to give way to a new rival at the Metropolitan —the longer, darker opera of the German school, fine in quality but less expensive to produce.

The Metropolitan's inaugural-night diva was the lyric soprano Christine Nilsson (*left*). No longer in her first youth, Nilsson still possessed the beauty for the role of Marguerite, and her mature art was rewarded with avalanches of flowers and golden ornaments. Opposite her appeared Italo Campanini (*lower left*), a dynamic tenor whose voice also showed some of the ravages of time but who for years to come could boast the title of "the most popular Faust who has ever sung in New York."

The New York opera public, now divided by the rivalry between the two opera houses—the Academy downtown and the Metropolitan far north of the residential center—was lured uptown by such popular singers as Nilsson, Campanini, and the baritone Del Puente, and by such lavish productions as Ponchielli's *La Gioconda,* the only opera of the season then new to New York. Thus, the Metropolitan won the day. Audiences revelled in its magnificent costumes from France, accepted its *Carmen* and *Lohengrin* in Italian translations, forgave its faulty orchestra, and approved its vigorous chorus. The new house soon became such a significant feature of the city's life that an artist's montage of its stellar audience was published (*next page*), fancifully depicting the nation's most prominent figures in politics, journalism, industry, society, and the stage, all shown together in the auditorium as if gathered for a single performance.

An artist's conception

1. Cornelius Vanderbilt
2. Mary Anderson
3. Mrs. Samuel Colgate
4. The Duchess of Marlborough
5. Mayor Hugh J. Grant
6. Mrs. Vanderbilt
7. James Gordon Bennett
8. Joseph Pulitzer
9. Mrs. Herman Oelrichs
10. Carl Schurz
11. Charles A. Dana
12. William Dean Howells
13. George W. Childs
14. Grover Cleveland
15. Jay Gould
16. George W. Curtis
17. Mrs. Astor
18. Unidentified
19. Mrs. Cleveland
20. Murat Halstead

of an 1891 Metropolitan audience

21. General Henry W. Slocum
22. Colonel Edward B. Fellows
23. Hamilton Fish
24. Unidentified
25. Edgar Saltus
26. John Wanamaker
27. James G. Blaine
28. Thomas B. Reed
29. Levi P. Morton
30. Mrs. Cooper Hewitt
31. Mrs. Potter Palmer
32. Edmund Stanton
33. F. Gray Griswold
34. Chauncey M. Depew
35. President Harrison
36. Mrs. Middleton Burrill
37. General T. W. Palmer
38. Bret Harte
39. Andrew Carnegie
40. Henry Villard
41. Mrs. Thomas M. Logan
42. Mrs. S. Dillon Ripley
43. Mrs. Adolph Ladenberg
44. William Henry Crane
45. Albert M. Palmer
46. John Jacob Astor
47. Ward McAllister
48. D. Ogden Mills
49. Unidentified
50. Edwin Booth
51. John Drew
52. Russell Sage
53. Dan Frohman
54. Henry Clews
55. Joseph Jefferson
56. Collis P. Huntington
57. Augustin Daly
58. Lillian Russell
59. Mrs. Albert Stevens

The Italian opera of the Metropolitan's first season was melodious, brightly lighted, decorative. You could whistle the tunes on the way home. The orchestra provided tinkling accompaniments and did not interfere with the singers. But Italian opera, with its high-priced stars and lavish settings, proved to be expensive entertainment. Thus Metropolitan stockholders, turning their backs on further deficits, reached to Germany for more modest fare.

The new Wagnerian repertory proved serious and usually somber. Its musical interest centered in the orchestra, which was fortunate since many of the German singers muttered or spluttered their guttural phrases. Only a few of them, like the heroic tenor Max Alvary (*left*), famed as Siegfried, and the soprano Lilli Lehmann (*right*), as renowned for her Italian roles as for her Brünnhilde, could combine vocal brilliance with the intense dramatic expression still reflected in their fading photographs.

Like Italian opera, German music drama, too, soon had its downfall, though for a different reason. Wagner's message was considered "cultural," but, as entertainment, it depended on intellectual participation from the audience, and many Metropolitan box holders were not accustomed to such demands. Even the newspapers of the day lampooned the struggle between the mythological heroes of Wagner and the romantic Italians.

THE WAR OF THE OPERAS

A HARMONIOUS BATTLE.

17

The operatic war between the Germans and the Italians ended, like Wagner's Ring Cycle, in a conflagration. As if taking its cue from the *Götterdämmerung* finale, the Metropolitan Opera House burst into flames on August 27, 1892. It had not been the heat of controversy, however, but ill-advised economy that had destroyed the building. In the days of gas jets and gauze scenery, many theaters had gone up in smoke. Memories of a hideous disaster in Vienna had caused the New York architect to utilize fireproof construction, install a sprinkler system, even add metal stage supports and an iron curtain.

In 1892, the company had suffered financial straits. To save money, labor, and time, the fire-prevention devices had been abandoned. In mid-summer, inflammable scenery was being painted on stage, and a workman's cigarette did the rest.

Out of the ashes of the Metropolitan a new phoenix arose: international opera. Under Henry Abbey's original management, the pattern had been set, but in that regime Faust had hailed Marguerite's cottage in a French tune to the Italian words *Salve dimora!,* while Lohengrin's Germanic swan had become a *cigno gentil.* When the lofty Wagnerian standards which had subsequently been introduced by Manager Leopold Damrosch were cut down by his death, his successor, the diplomatic Edmund Stanton, continued to offer German opera. The galleries applauded; but the boxes dozed and chattered. Only Italian opera could titillate the tiaras. The compromise introduced by Mr. Abbey, who returned after the fire with two partners, Edward Schoeffel and Maurice Grau, was novel: performances in two or three languages at once. Lovers wooed in French and were answered in Italian.

Only when Maurice Grau took over the reins alone in 1898 did a valid international opera emerge. So many of the top-flight singers had by that time acquired experience in Europe that they were now able to present opera in the language of the composer. Thus, shortly after the first flash photograph was taken in the opera house in 1895 (*next page*), a consistent policy of opera in the original language had been accepted. Now, in its so-called Golden Age, the Metropolitan lacked only professional stagecraft—a skill it was later to find in the manager Heinrich Conried.

HENRY E. ABBEY
1883-1884, 1891-1896

LEOPOLD DAMROSCH
1884-1885

EDMUND STANTON
1885-1891

MAURICE GRAU
1896-1903

HEINRICH CONRIED
1903-1908

The Dawn

of a Golden Age

Evidence is not lacking of the golden quality of opera at the turn of the century. Elderly opera-lovers still speak of singers who, like great ladies and gentlemen, rehearsed in gloves and top hats and surrounded themselves with maids and valets. The primitive phonograph records of that day still echo with voices under absolute control: Plançon's agility in the bass register, Melba's icy, flute-like perfection, Nordica's silver-throated magnificence, and Emma Eames's flawless vocal production. The old photographs of these singers convince us that here were statuesque men and women, their appearance tailored to the taste of the salon. The artists traveled with their own costumes in their own monumental trunks, their traditions of stage business secure in their well-coiffed heads. The only function of the conductor was to trim their orchestral accompaniment. The impresario existed chiefly to arbitrate their feuds. To these singers, discipline meant only the arduous training of their distant youth. They were stars, magnificent and imperious, set in self-determined orbits, accepting gracious invitations to sing a given role on a given date, sending a secretary to represent them at rehearsal.

One singer, Marcella Sembrich (*right*), spanned so long a career that she seems to typify three distinct eras: the inaugural season of the Metropolitan, its Golden Age, and the dawn of our own day. As a girl in her twenties, Sembrich revealed her musicianship as Lucia, and as Violetta in *La Traviata*. She returned in the 1890's to compete on even terms with the heroic voices of the day through the perfection of her skillful and charming comedy as Rosina in *Il Barbiere di Siviglia* and as Zerlina in *Don Giovanni*. She did not withdraw from the opera stage until 1909, leaving a legacy of velvet softness and ripe artistic intelligence to all opera-lovers.

It is the fashion today to decry the great singers of the past and to laugh at the snobbery that surrounded them. Even the metal of their voices is compared unfavorably to the more natural vocalism of our own day. But we forget that the public of the nineties did not ask for stage illusion or for the identification which is implicit in the realistic subjects of modern musical drama. In the lyric theater, social revelations and interpretations of history were of little concern. Instead, audiences clamored for the full impact of Edouard de Reszke's sardonic Méphistophélès. They could idealize Tristan and Roméo in Jean de Reszke. They shivered with delight at Nellie Melba's marble Juliette, at the radiant clarity of Lillian Nordica's Kundry, and at the polished beauty of Emma Eames as Aida. The "nights of the seven stars" (as Golden Age performances were called when such artists as Victor Maurel, Sofia Scalchi, and Pol Plançon were added to the cast) shone in a galaxy of brilliance that seems to us today as remote as the stars in the sky.

Golden Age stars: Edouard de Reszke as Méphistophélès (left), his brother Jean as Tristan (above), Nellie Melba as Juliette (top), Lillian Nordica as Kundry (right), and Emma Eames as Aida

ater *to yield to the splendors of Sherry's restaurant*

reat singers have traditionally attracted controversy. Under the management of Heinrich Conried, not only the singers but the operas themselves became the subject of scandal. In spite of the compelling gifts of Olive Fremstad in the title role (*left*), *Salome* proved abhorrent to the 1907 audiences because of its bold sensuality and realistic horror. At the command of the stockholders, Oscar Wilde's degenerate princess was banished from the repertory, as recorded in a cartoon of the day (*below*). Even the glistening musical raiment of Richard Strauss had not been considered an adequate dress. Then Conried achieved greater re-

nown with another kind of scandal. Defying the monopoly of Wagner's heirs, who wished to reserve *Parsifal* for their theater in Bayreuth, and overriding the pleas of the clergy and the petitions of the squeamish, who felt it a sacrilege to present a religious drama in a theater, he staged the work at the Metropolitan many times during his first season at the opera house, successfully flaunting it in the face of his critics.

These scandals were soon forgotten. What had been considered blasphemy by the clergy immediately became an annual Good Friday ritual to devout laymen. But the stage antics of certain operatic personalities already in the company caused further criticism to be heaped on the head of Conried. To Henry Krehbiel, most eminent of New York music critics, Emma Calvé, most popular of all Carmens (*right*), seemed "a woman thoroughly wanton and diabolically equipped with wicked witcheries." To a Boston critic, she was "an instrument blown by the lips of passion." To Philadelphia, she suggested "snakes and subtlety." Even the great Feodor Chaliapin, a fresh importation of Conried, was described as "bestiality incarnate" at his debut in Boito's *Mefistofele* and accused of distasteful gestures in his performance as Don Basilio in *Il Barbiere di Siviglia*.

31

*The beautiful young
Geraldine Farrar,
soon to become one
of Gatti-Casazza's
greatest stars,
made a golden debut
at the close
of the Golden Age*

The Reign
of Gatti-Casazza

The new general manager of 1908, Giulio Gatti-Casazza, enriched the Metropolitan with major artistic assets: his own professional acumen and personal cultivation. He also brought the man who was to become the greatest conductor of the generation, Arturo Toscanini. Losing the treasury of Golden Age stars, Gatti still found on the roster not only the soprano Geraldine Farrar, whose emotionally vibrant voice and magnetic personality were to bring the city to her feet, but also the tenor whose matchless music came to mean opera to the world: Enrico Caruso. What if Caruso is remembered as a clown whose antics extended down to the point of his pencil as a cartoonist? He was the clown whose heart is breaking, the classical figure that leaps through the circus hoop into the heart of man. Masters of discipline, Gatti and his Maestro also raised their stars to new eminence.

An historic trio:
Gatti-Casazza (seated),
Toscanini, and Farrar
confer on the set
of Madame Sans-Gêne

In the Golden Age of the Metropolitan, the stars of opera had burst on the stage in full-blown glory. In the reign of Gatti, they were developed and molded by the management. The greatest of them all, Caruso, now grew from a lyric tenor "with tiresome Italian vocal affectations" into a tireless artist, as renowned for his majestic impersonations of Samson and John of Leyden and Eleazar as for the unmatched beauty and dimension of his apparently effortless singing.

From an earlier day, the velvet-voiced Louise Homer remained to add new overtones to her art. The smooth baritone voice of Antonio Scotti's youth darkened with time, but the compelling suavity of his Scarpia owed much to Toscanini's vision. Ernestine Schumann-Heink, another veteran, reappeared over the Gatti years, the tonal color of her former days now shaded with eerie eloquence. Newcomers of the regime are remembered for a variety of endowments: Emmy Destinn for her great power and flexibility, Pasquale Amato for his convincing style, Frances Alda for her vocal agility and appealing impersonations, Margarete Matzenauer for the lusciousness of her entire range.

The only Metropolitan impresario who did not speak fluent English, Gatti was nevertheless the first to present American opera, the first to develop the American singer. Riccardo Martin

proved to be a romantic figure and Orville Harrold a subtle vocalist, while Rosa Ponselle rose from vaudeville to become the most mellifluous Norma and Leonora in the history of the house. The daughter of a member of his own stage crew, Claudia Muzio (*left*), rose to stardom as a conscientious and tasteful artist.

When Toscanini, Caruso, and Farrar departed from the scene, they were replaced by the cream of the European crop: the resonant tenor Giovanni Martinelli and his silky-voiced colleague, Beniamino Gigli, who shared Caruso's roles; Maria Jeritza, who gave life to a dozen heroines with her fascination; Amelita Galli-Curci, who proved that vocal acrobatics can at the same time be mellow; and, eventually, the unforgettable Lotte Lehmann, as gifted an actress as a singer. Chaliapin returned, not this time to offend the squeamish subscribers, but, instead, to awe them with his recreation of the imperial Russia of *Boris Godunov.* Tetrazzini flashed across a single season with blinding brilliance. Lucrezia Bori disseminated irresistible charm to ear and eye through a long career. Frieda Hempel reminded her hearers of the *bel canto* of the Golden Age; Alma Gluck offered a whiff of ethereal tone. The giant Leo Slezak established a tradition with his powerful Otello. The silvery sopranos of Elisabeth Rethberg and Florence

Easton, the magnificence of Karin Branzell's contralto, the fluent style of Giuseppe DeLuca, and the sonorous low notes of Clarence Whitehill, Adamo Didur, and Leon Rothier—all of these brought pleasure to the public. Unlike the Golden Age, this era no longer saw starlight focus on a few legendary voices; instead, an entire production glowed with diffused intensity. The conductors took a cue from Toscanini, demanding more authority. The art of the stage director evolved.

Meanwhile, another golden tide was running out. The increasing pinch of the income tax was followed by the pressures of a falling stock market. The reserves of a more prosperous day were tapped to meet mounting deficits. The American novelties did not hold the stage, Deems Taylor's *Peter Ibbetson,* alone among these, enduring into a fourth season. The public did not respond to Gatti's Italian novelties and compared the performances of standard works to happier days. Operatic production was growing more costly. Eventually Gatti-Casazza withdrew to Italy, unwilling to cope with the new conditions.

Yet the assets assembled by Gatti proved of real worth in the future. A few of his younger artists were working their way up to glory, among them Ezio Pinza and Lawrence Tibbett. Lily Pons had barely started her scintillant parade of damsels in distress, and the great Kirsten Flagstad was already at hand, with Lauritz Melchior as her perfect partner in the Wagnerian music dramas.

Gatti's stars: Antonio Scotti's Falstaff (left), Lucrezia Bori's Juliette (far right), Chaliapin's Boris (upper right), Tetrazzini's Lucia (lower right). Above, top to bottom: Frieda Hempel's Marschallin, Emmy Destinn's Aida, Alma Gluck's Mimi

In 1920, Orville Harrold's Parsifal succumbed to the wiles
of Margarete Matzenauer as Kundry.

From 1909 to 1913, Leo Slezak's Otello
towered over Frances Alda's frail Desdemona

Rosa Ponselle's sinister Margared in Le Roi d'Ys *(left); top, left to right, Galli-Curci's Violetta, Louise Homer's Amneris, Gigli's Vasco da Gama. Above: Jeritza's Elisabeth, Lotte Lehmann's Marschallin (bottom), and DeLuca's Figaro*

Transi

on and Triumph

In the early thirties, opera was entering a new era. The box holders were dying, season subscribers were ebbing away, the elegance was fading. But a new manager arrived—the singer Edward Johnson, whose popular characterization of Peter Ibbetson suggested his own gallantry.

Great Wagner performances, the first popular presentations of Mozart, a team of impressive conductors, and fresh opportunities for the American singer—these were the most important contributions of Eddie Johnson's regime. The Scandinavian countries, little touched by World War I, supplied the singers for the Nibelung sagas. The golden metal of Kirsten Flagstad's voice, with her tender yet majestic interpretations, the heroic voice of Lauritz Melchior, seconded by Karin Branzell and Kerstin Thorborg against the bass voices of Emanuel List and Alexander Kipnis and the baritones Friedrich Schorr and Herbert Janssen—these revitalized the Wagnerian dramas.

It was a new Mozart era, too. Johnson's revivals of *Figaro, Don Giovanni,* and *The Magic Flute* profited by the sonorous voice of Ezio Pinza, the secure charm of Bidu Sayao, and the lyric beauty of Zinka Milanov and Eleanor Steber.

*Few operas
were so popular
in the forties
as Mozart's*
Le Nozze di Figaro

51

U nder the great conductors of the Johnson era—Bruno Walter, Fritz Reiner, Sir Thomas Beecham among them—the less experienced American singers, too, enjoyed new opportunities for success. Some of these, like Lawrence Tibbett, worked their way from the ranks to stardom. Grace Moore (*below, right*), trailing her adoring public from operetta and the movies, won them to opera. Helen Traubel (*far right*) rose to replace Flagstad in Valhalla. European-born artists, in turn, came to look upon the United States as their home. Pinza (*left*) became as famous for his Broadway appearance in *South Pacific* as for his Metropolitan successes. Lily Pons (*below*) and Giovanni Martinelli (*below, center*) never lost their foreign speaking accents, but were accepted as American idols.

53

omething that was pretentious was receding from the world of opera. The opera-goers who were lampooned by Reginald Marsh were chicly haggard in youth and portly with age, hung with ermine and diamonds, with opera glasses trained on each other as eagerly as on the stage. But even within the opera house itself, many changes were taking place. Soon after Marsh's satirical painting was completed, the second row of boxes was abolished, and a more democratic usage prevailed in the reconstruction of the Grand Tier, which now became the most desirable of the balconies.

Though the old regime lingered on, bridging the gulf between past and present, a new and younger public was infiltrating the opera world. They flocked to the Wagnerian appearances of Flagstad and Melchior, the Mozart performances of Pinza and Sayao, the English-language presentations of such unfamiliar Russian operas as Rimsky-Korsakov's *Coq d'Or* and Mussorgsky's *Khovanchina*.

Through the Saturday radio broadcasts and the development of long-playing recordings, the newcomers heard grand opera in their homes. Here they could follow score or libretto, learning much that might elude observers in the theater. Opera was recognized no longer as mere luxurious entertainment for the few but essential culture for the many. The means to share it were at hand.

A major factor in the new attitude was the influence of The Metropolitan Opera Guild, founded by Mrs. August Belmont to broaden the base of responsibility for the Opera Association and to increase public knowledge and appreciation of the art. Gala nights still attracted a luxurious public to the opera house itself, but, for special matinees, a new type of audience, drawn from the high schools of the city and surrounding communities, came to fill the theater. Never before had such a varied American public enjoyed opera.

Exhibitions, displays, lectures, and a variety of publications were organized by the Guild. Meetings were held at the opera house at which pictures of stars of the past were displayed on a screen with the historic voices demonstrated by amplified recordings. Tours backstage, lectures on unfamiliar works, art contests, ticket and libretto service facilities, radio programs—these were a few of the dozens of separate projects involved in the Guild's varied program.

In 1952, Mrs. Belmont created the National Council of the Metropolitan Opera Association, a nation-wide organization whose energies are devoted to regional auditions for Metropolitan aspirants, a Central Opera Service for the guidance and assistance of local opera companies, and the contribution of funds for many new—and often highly successful—Metropolitan productions.

The traditions of grand opera have foreshadowed its present state, recurring like themes half-heard, half-forgotten. But the traditions are changing and broadening. A new type of impresario has arisen to meet the age. The ingenious speculators, the professional musicians, the imperious potentates of the past seem outmoded. The genial tenor who could smile and make do in hard times is gone. From the worlds of music management and merchandising has come a new man, Rudolf Bing, educated in the theater and now reaching for new dramatic values from the spoken stage. The imaginative direction of Margaret Webster, the finesse of Alfred Lunt, and the deft timing of Cyril Ritchard have been added to the sound experience of Herbert Graf. Operas have changed the period and locale of their settings with the varied fantasy of Rolf Gérard and the architectural conceptions of Eugene Berman. In the first ten years of the Bing regime, nine-tenths of the repertory exhibited a new dress. Costumes were conceived not as a heterogeneous mixture of personal preferences but as a unified display invented by the same imagination that was responsible for the stage decor.

And Now...

THE GLITTER

NG PRESENT

The Metropolitan today officially recognizes no favorites among its stars. In Europe, Rudolf Bing discovered the honeyed beauty of Victoria de los Angeles, the silvery power of Renata Tebaldi, the many-colored tones of Maria Callas, the artistic strength of Birgit Nilsson, the agility and security of Leonie Rysanek, the luscious loveliness of Lisa Della Casa, and the trumpet tones of Mario Del Monaco. Bing developed the local discoveries of the Johnson era: Eleanor Steber's intensity, the dark warmth of Risë Stevens, Richard Tucker's heroic tenor, and the rich power of Leonard Warren and Robert Merrill. He also found fresh American talents: the pure soprano of Lucine Amara, the dramatic sincerity of Rosalind Elias, the velvet sonority of Jean Madeira, the authority of George London, the poetic appeal of Theodor Uppman, and the high artistic standard of Giorgio Tozzi.

63

Standees at the rail, hostesses in the boxes,
and white-shirted clubmen in the Grand Tier

. await the overture

What is opera today? It is still the glamor of spectacle and the irresistible appeal of great voices, exciting personalities, and floods of symphonic sound. But, beyond these indispensable elements, the appeal of opera lies in its magical moments of identification, when the listener becomes one with the artist, when both are possessed by the same emotion—an emotion raised to new significance. The master of this transformation is the conductor, whose baton holds sway over a hundred musicians and 3,500 opera-lovers. He unlocks the doors into a world of great moments in which the color and motion of the spectacle, the glory of the music, and the inspired art of the interpreter are fused into one ennobling experience.

At the conductor's beat,
the world of everyday fades,
giving way to the magic
of the great world of opera . . .

*. . . a world of love
and patriotism
such as this moment
from Aida when father
pleads with daughter
to save their country*

. . . a world of pageantry when stagecraft merges dance and music as in the Triumphal Scene of Aida

Magic in the Making

To produce the physical magic of a masterpiece like *Aida* requires hard work. The majesty of ancient Thebes is reduced to strips of wood and yards of canvas in the morning light, cluttering the Seventh Avenue sidewalk as the warehouse crew packs it off to storage. Round the clock work the stagehands, a team coached on a split-second schedule to dress the stage before every scene and strike the set the instant the curtain falls. For the magic of opera depends on more than the waving of a wand, even if it is the conductor's, on more than the skill of the stage director. It involves hundreds of people carrying on their tasks in four languages, driven to peak efficiency after sunset.

*With Aida's
first scene in place (left)
and all Egypt
stacked on stage,
a lone stagehand relaxes
before the rise
of the evening's curtain*

74

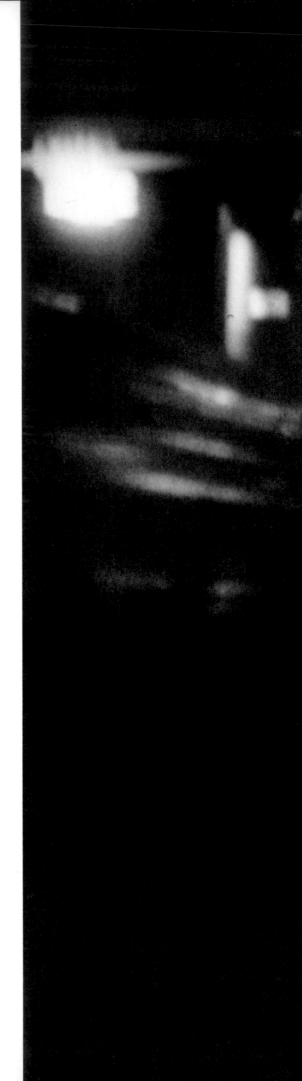

The conductor
is a lonely man
dreaming
of a perfection
that always
floats beyond him

Stage manager
and stage director
create a court
or village crowd
from the chorus
by the magic
of suggestion,
imprecation,
or encouragement

*The director teaches swordplay
to a young singer. A dozen technicians
preside over every stage rehearsal*

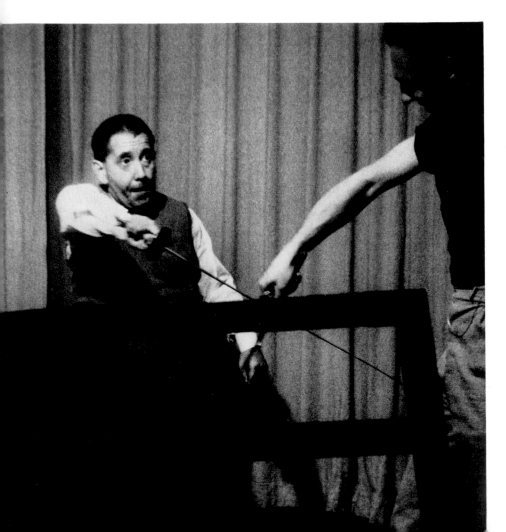

B ad rehearsals, according to legend, mean good performances. Can it be that the exasperation of the stage director—the final passionate gesture of frustration—is needed to rouse the cast into flame? The expert uses a gamut of techniques: praise, blame, challenge, taunt, and prayer. Some newcomers from the spoken stage rely on their skill as actors to inspire an effect. Some of them probe the instincts of the artists in front of them. Sometimes the cool and lucid approach is sufficient. More often, one man must rise to fever pitch in order that a hundred others may glow with white heat. Then paint, powder, plaster, and canvas, as well as workaday singers and weary dancers who have waited for hours for their moment of glory, may burst into the conflagration that is grand opera.

*Two great dancers
of the past
mold the talents
of a new generation*

The ballet used to be called the orphan of the opera world, for it appears momentarily, usually at the climax of the drama, and concludes so rapidly that the public is hardly aware of its detailed construction. It takes seven years of schooling for a dancer to prepare for the *corps de ballet*. Each day starts with thirty minutes of exercises at the bar to limber and warm up the muscles. The same exercises are then repeated without support in the center of a large rehearsal room. Choreography, the pattern of a given dance, does not enter into the picture until the dancer has completed the seven years' schooling. Just as the aria is the objective of the vocal student, impatient with her scales, so choreography is the goal to which the dancer must aspire. Until the dancer is actually on stage, the exercises persist, in the dressing rooms, in the wings. The rigors continue even through the preparation for a given ballet, all focused on a few moments of glamorous motion on the stage.

The moment when

grace and beauty

seem to defy

the laws of gravity

and human weakness

Opera magic is brewed from many solid substances as well as from such evanescent elements as light and music. Giant masks contribute to the gruesomeness of *Macbeth's* witches. Pails of pigment and smoking cauldrons of "fix" wait on the paint bridge for the scenic artists to transform drops and borders into the semblance of satin or velvet, sunset skies, hillside villages, or subterranean prisons carved from gigantic granite blocks.

Paint is an important item on the face, too. More than an hour is required to change a stalwart young bass-baritone into Boris Godunov, the shattered Czar of all the Russias. Newcomers are taught the latest techniques by the professional make-up artist. Soon they catch on: even the young dancers who prepared to be clowns or gypsies peer into their mirrors as they scrub their noses with paper tissue and look to their kits for the magic greases and powders that have disguised their identity and will now bring them back to the world of everyday.

The costuming of opera casts a variety of spells. It sets the period, determines the rank, accents the personality. But it does more. It clothes the uncertainties of the modern human being with the assurance of the artist. The preening tenor takes on the bold bluster of the Drum Major in *Wozzeck*; the casual, sportive young bass becomes Don Giovanni, the irresistible lover of all the ages.

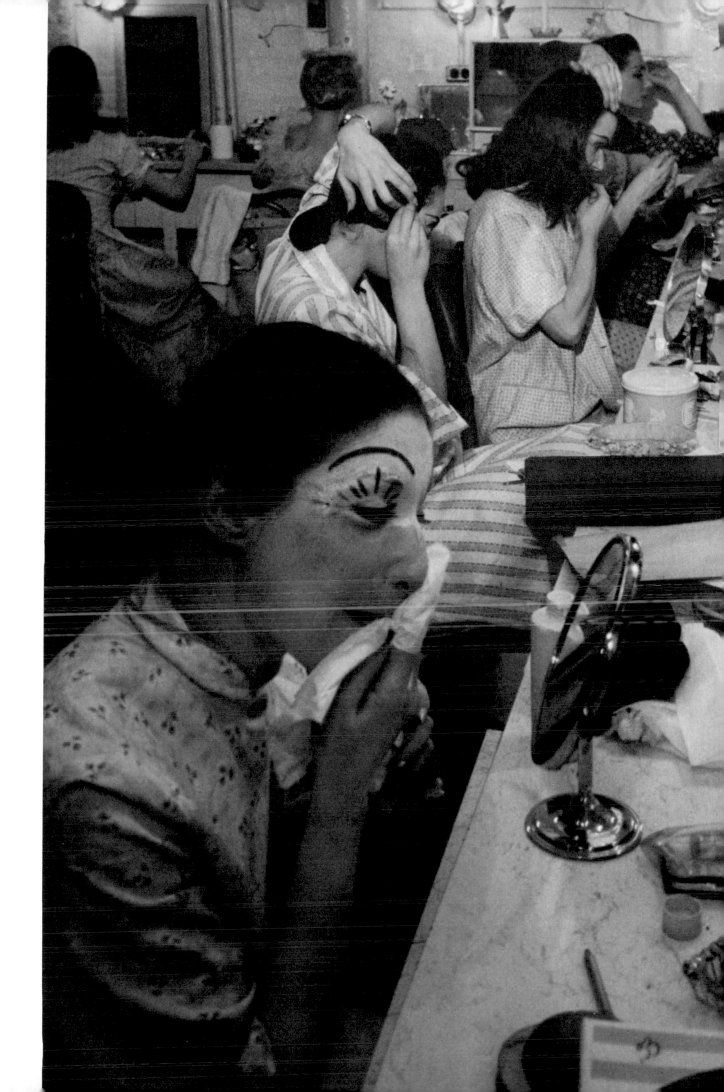

Costumes in the wardrobe: inert yardage;
on the singer: protection from himself,
transformation to heroism or villainy

The tenor preens,
tries his voice,
surveys his medals,
and becomes
the dazzling
Drum Major
of Berg's Wozzeck

The tenor looks to his uniform for the assurance of rank, but the child bridges the gulf between reality and illusion with no effort at all. How does the chubby American girl transform herself into the tragic little boy born to Wozzeck and his Marie? Here the process is half completed: a costume, make-up, mirror are all in place. But the child is still smiling at the transformation, not yet ready for the inner change that must arrive before that devastating moment in the last scene when it learns of the death of its parents and tries to hide its misery.

A score of technicians are at hand to help. A stage manager will shepherd the little actress on stage. A prompter will mouth her cue. The orchestra will depress or exhilarate her as the score demands. She may rub her nose ruefully at her familiar appearance now, but by some mysterious magic she is almost ready for the metamorphosis.

The stage manager waits for the signal to raise the curtain. The prompter, squeezed into his eerie, coffin-like box, will soon become the singer's best friend

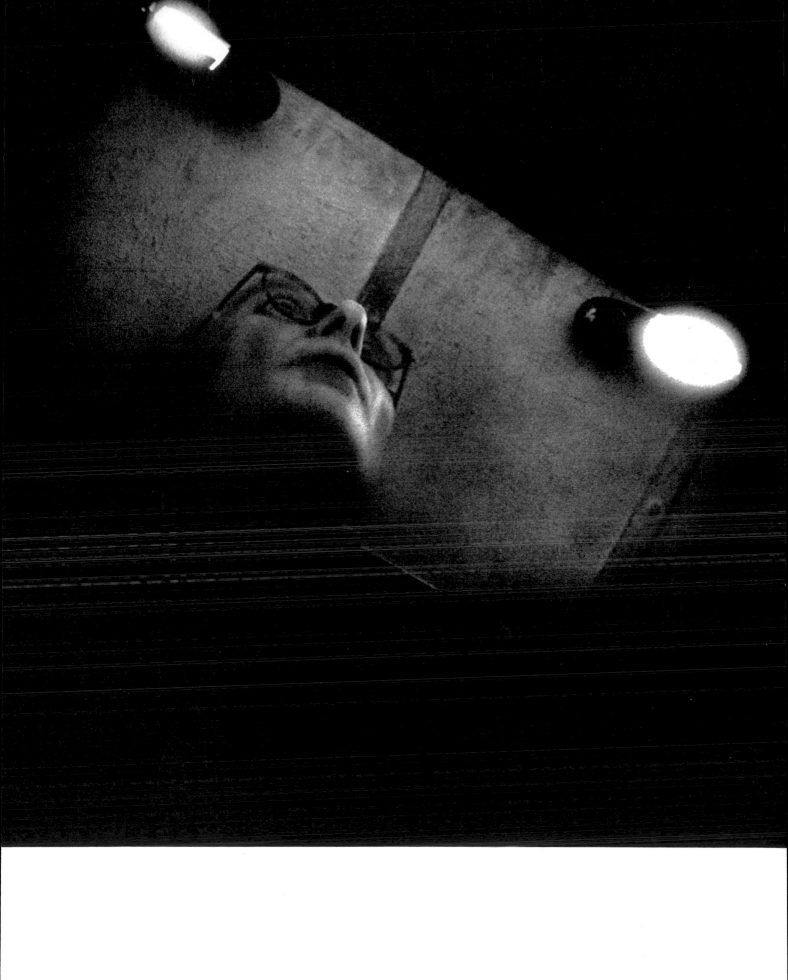

As the first notes of the orchestra set the mood of the drama,

the conductor's baton throbs with a special magic

The
Great Moments

Scenery is in place, make-up and costumes are in order, the prompter is crouched under his hood, the orchestra has sounded, and a great moment is at hand. The popularity of certain operas seems to defy time and space. Styles in music change. Great singing actors come and go. Productions grow obsolete. But the great moments retain their impact. They arise from the inspiration of genius.

There are moments which point at the identity of man and mask, proclaiming that the stage is itself the world. There are moments which bring to life an enduring issue in a forgotten page of history. Great moments may speak through laughter, through harsh realism, through sheer cascades of tone. They may emerge from any era, from distant or familiar lands, arrayed in Roman togas, medieval armor, oriental robes, or sack suits. The only similarity among great operatic moments lies in the emotional response which they evoke.

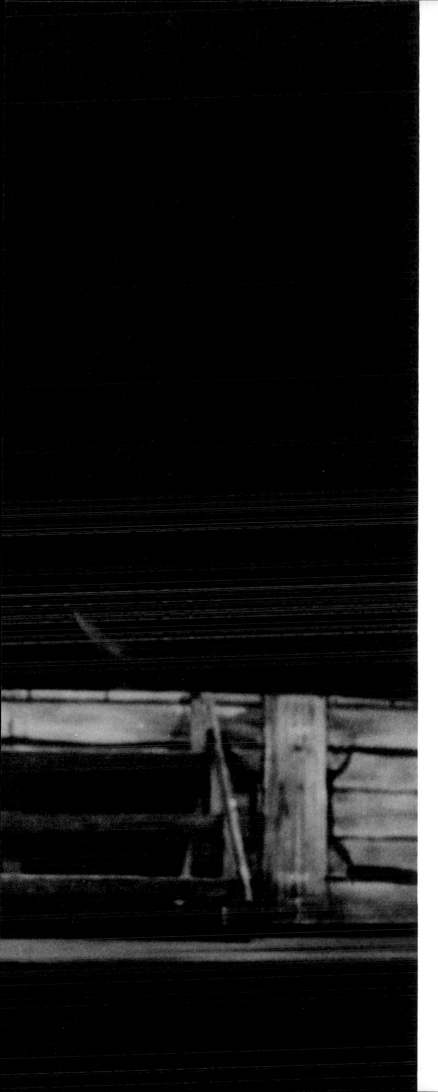

The despairing hero in Pagliacci, *robbed of his wife's love, cannot hide his anguish in the powdered grimace of the clown*

The triumphant serenity of Cavalleria Rusticana's Easter Hymn

…contrasts with the torture of the excommunicated Santuzza

The passionate gypsy
Carmen, interrupted
in her fight with
another cigarette
factory worker,
resists arrest
at the hands of the
brigadier Don José

Happiness echoes pitifully in Madame Butterfly's voice
as she scatters rose petals about the room where she
will vainly await her faithless husband until the dawn

The flirtatious ladies of Così fan tutte, *gathered in their garden*

ugh at the ridiculous advances of their disguised suitors

*Her marriage
to Figaro promises
a joyous future
to Susanna (left).
The hysterical
pursuit of pleasure
offers escape
to La Traviata's
frail heroine (right)*

Another Violetta
raises her glass
to toast the joys
of the moment
and the fleeting
pleasures of love

A raging Isolde calls upon the elements for vengeance against the man she had once loved

The cobbler poet Hans Sachs (left) accepts the praise of the

Nuremberg guilds, old mastersingers and young apprentices alike

The dream figure of Lohengrin,
knight of the Grail, appears
in a vision to the maiden Elsa,
who prays for a champion
who will defend her from evil

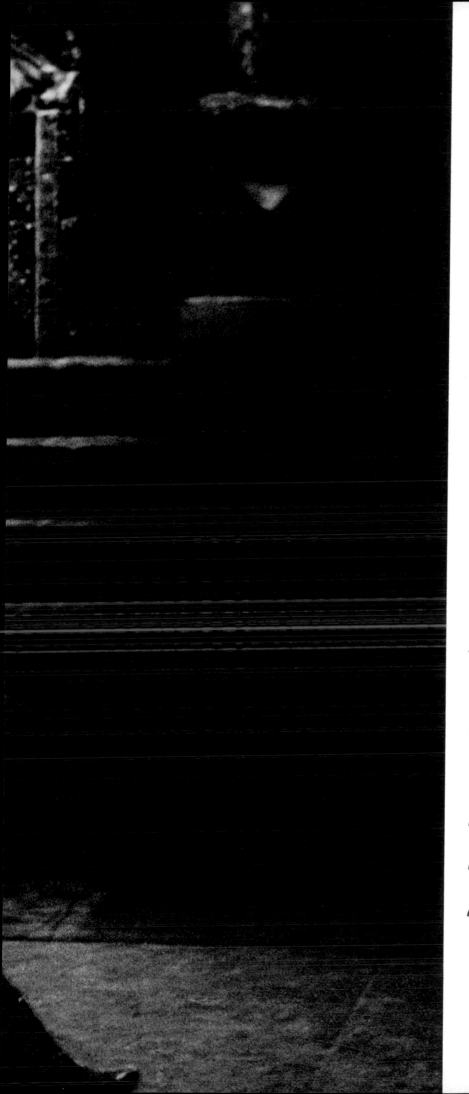

As crafty boyars plot
for the succession
to the throne of Russia,
a dying Boris Godunov,
haunted by guilt
and obsessed by fear
of his enemies,
asks God to forgive him

*A Don Giovanni's
last, defiant fling
is enlivened
by wine and women*

The cunning vengeance
of Baron Scarpia
foils Tosca and her lover,
pursuing them to death
in a Roman prison

Between the Acts

The excitements of grand opera demand interruption and relaxation between the frenzied tensions of the drama. Without some pause, the singers could not survive the strain on their voices, nor could the players maintain their skill, nor the audience its pitch of feverish excitement.

What happens backstage during intermission? This is the time when the stage crew springs into action, dodging the departing cast. It is also the moment when artists and chorus, hoisting skirts and swords, hurry to their dressing rooms for a change of costume, a sip at the water cooler, or merely the touch of a rabbit's foot which will freshen the melting grease paint.

The casual public strolls into Sherry's restaurant for refreshment or struggles through the crowd into the bar for a drink or into the outer lobbies for a smoke. At such times it is possible to find some elderly opera-lovers pointing out the portraits of their idols to a younger generation, or students examining those autographs of the composers and artists of the past which adorn the lobbies, or random members of the audience gazing at the jewels of historic prima donnas as the diamonds flash from museum cabinets in the foyer. At such moments also, it is possible to observe a few quiet ones remaining in their seats on every level of the building to let the performance of the evening sink into their hearts and their memories.

Three youn

pera-goers create a modern, though timeless, Metropolitan vignette

Some stragglers remain in the lobby
while a maid sits on watch, guarding the Parterre boxes

New Perspectives

One of opera's oldest traditions is that the public is always waiting for something new—and at the same time resisting it. A rarely-heard work like Verdi's half-forgotten *Macbeth*; a first opera, *Vanessa,* by a well-known symphonic composer, Samuel Barber, and a skillful librettist like Gian-Carlo Menotti; a bitter social commentary, *Wozzeck,* by one of the pioneers of modern music, Alban Berg—such unfamiliar operas invite yet defy instant approval.

In the opera world, people love what they know, mistrust what is strange. But in recent years, these three experiments—a familiar story in a familiar idiom but a new form, a new story in a romantic mood, and a realistic story set to the atonal music of the twenties—have all sounded an offbeat challenge to the lovers of *Aida, Carmen,* and *Lohengrin.* What verdict for an unfamiliar work? The director can only knock wood . . . and hope.

Lady Macbeth's candle-lit sleepwalking scene gains fresh horror from the fireworks of Verdi's score

An impetuous Vanessa
spurns the stranger
who has come
to her snowbound estate
in place of
her long-lost lover

The misery of a war-torn world shows little effect on the children of Wozzeck, whose soldier-hero is driven to madness by an insane doctor and a sadistic captain

Curtain Call

In front of the great gold curtain, the doctor of *Wozzeck* drops his maniacal hysteria and returns to the smiling normalcy of the artist. His impersonation has melted away. But a new and more speedy metamorphosis is taking place. Midway in the brief journey back to reality, before the actor has quite become a man, he appears in full costume to receive the homage of the public. Sometimes a soprano is so shaken by the frenzy of her role that she has been known to stand trembling as she clutches the edge of the curtain. Sometimes tears may come to her eyes. Once in a decade, the audience will demand a speech, and the singer may blurt out some half-heard thanks.

In the old days, flowers were hurled from the balconies, gifts were heaped in the wings. Today, such observances are limited to the stage door and the dressing rooms. But the curtain call continues. And as one traces the timings of opera performances across the years, one finds that some favorites have considerably delayed the dimming of the house lights by the length of the applause and by the number of bows demanded of them—and given.

Here the sinister Ortrud, evil genius of the mystical opera *Lohengrin,* seems released from her black jealousy and hatred as she is called back to the smiling world of a performance finished and a job well done. Artists vary in their manner in front of the curtain. Europeans are likely to sink into a deep court curtsey or a low bow from the hips. Some singers rely on an intimate little nod of the head. Many kiss the hands or fling their arms wide apart. A few wave at friends in adjacent boxes. Almost all of them smile. None of them has made the complete readjustment to reality. Why should they? That will come soon enough.

For the moment, for one last breathless moment, the singer floats on the echoes of applause before retiring into the everyday world of cleansing creams and autographs, the trip back to the hotel, and the agonizing wait for the daily newspapers and their fateful words of praise or blame.

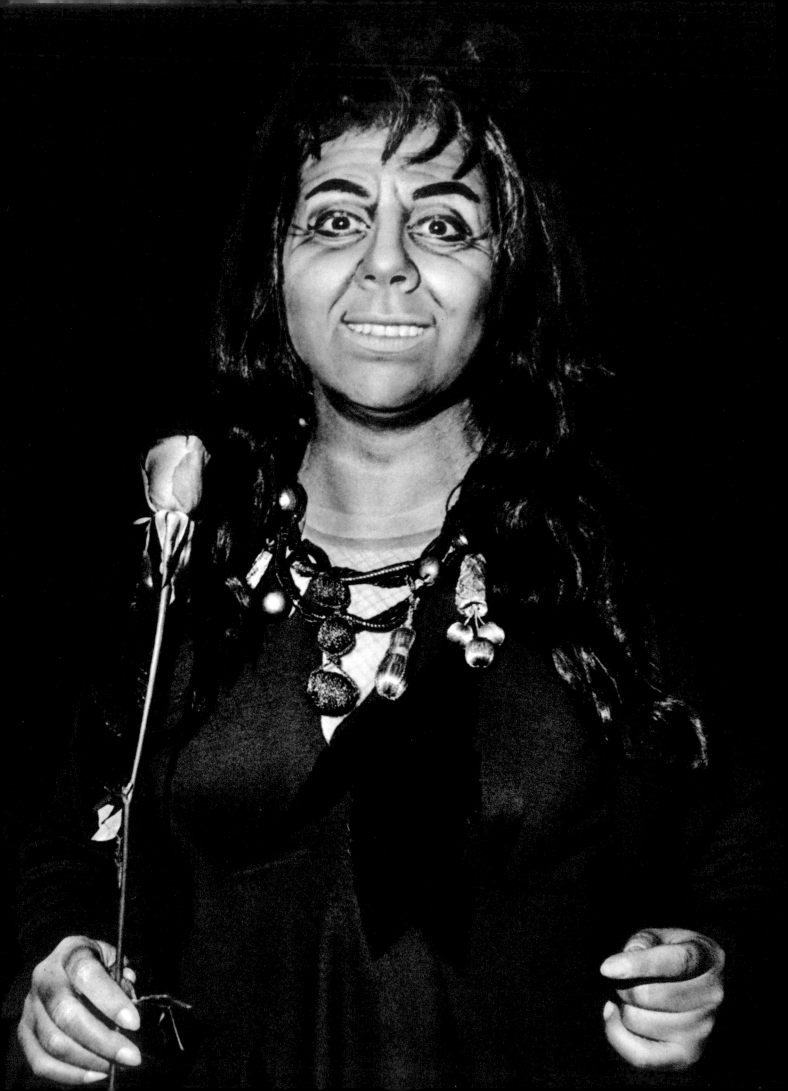

The euphoria of a great performance endures for some time. A smile of inner satisfaction may survive even the hideous lines and wrinkles of an old gypsy's make-up. Azucena's young fingers hold a rose, symbolic of the tributes that are piled in her dressing room. Her two passionate arias have roused the house to wild and prolonged applause. Her nostalgic duet at the close of *Il Trovatore* showed no signs of fatigue, and her final imprecation, "You have killed your brother, my mother is avenged at last," rose to its high B-flat with flawless intonation and trumpet power.

Now the public throngs out again to Broadway, past the glittering marquee. The artist sinks into a cab. She has left her hat box, perhaps, for the wardrobe mistress to care for in the deserted dressing room. One by one, the house lights are extinguished, and a new ghostliness fills the opera house. Only a bit of litter, a pair of ballet slippers tossed aside and forgotten by some careless dancer, a folded newspaper, a torn program, remain.

As lights go out,
the old house
seems to dwarf
its new neighbors

Every night opera becomes a memory. Every day its performances go down into the long history that was born of the legends of Greek drama. Opera at the Metropolitan started as an Italian sugar plum. It survived the conflict of the German years and took on a high nobility from their tradition. It gathered the greatest voices of the world but became more than a galaxy of stars: it became a rich amalgam of metals mined in many lands. It put genius on the podium and art on the stage.

Operatic history looks to the daily record for facts and figures, but it finds its true meaning in human minds and hearts. In these minds the memories, sharp and clear at first, for good or bad, weaken and blur and melt into the background. Only a few survive in a single mind, and only a very few of them claim immortality. Caruso has reached the rank of a silver statue and a pile of biographies. The Metropolitan itself will doubtless be torn down; someday its site may even lose its identity, as in the case of the venerable Academy of Music which has given its name to a motion picture theater not at its own site but across the street from where it stood. But, like the expanding ring of water in a pool that is said to endure to infinity, some sound waves from the old house will echo through the halls of time. For such a stream of greatness, there can be no exit.

Picture Captions and Credits

PAGES

FRONTISPIECE:

This remarkable view of the stage and auditorium of the Metropolitan Opera House was taken during the performance of *Don Giovanni* given on the evening of April 8, 1958. To make this picture possible, the auditorium lights were turned on during a performance for the first time in the history of the house. The photograph was obtained through use of a special camera, equipped with a "fish-eye" lens and fastened to the center of the Family Circle railing.—*Ralph Morse*-Life, © *1958 Time Inc.*

4-5 The Goldman collection of autographed letters and musical manuscripts lines the foyer adjacent to the Thirty-ninth Street entrance of the opera house. Here are to be found autographs of composers from Johann Sebastian Bach (1685-1750) to Igor Stravinsky (1882-   ). The collection contains one of the few happy letters written to his father by the young Mozart and the only autographed letter of Modest Mussorgsky accessible to the U.S. public. The Goldman collection, which takes its name from the late Edwin Franko Goldman, who gave it to the Metropolitan in custody of The Metropolitan Opera Guild, was actually originated by Mr. Goldman's uncle, the late Nahan Franko, a Metropolitan conductor at the turn of the century. Recent additions have been made through the efforts of the Guild's memorabilia chairman, Mrs. O'Donnell Hoover.—*Photo by Gjon Mili.*

6-7 LEFT: The opening-night audience on October 27, 1958. The opera on that occasion was Puccini's *Tosca,* with Renata Tebaldi, Mario Del Monaco, and George London in the leading roles.—*Photo by Gjon Mili.*

RIGHT: An artist's delineation of subscribers arriving at the Academy of Music, predecessor of the Metropolitan Opera House, which stood on the north side of East Fourteenth Street in New York City, a site later occupied by the Consolidated Edison Company. The Academy was built in 1854, destroyed by fire in 1866, reopened the following year, and was finally demolished in 1926. It reached its operatic heyday from 1878 to 1886 under the administration of Col. James H. Mapleson. This drawing was probably executed about 1873.—*From The Bettmann Archive.*

8-9 LEFT: Metropolitan Opera House box holders await their carriages in the Thirty-ninth Street lobby of the house in 1894. The drawing was done by T. de Thulstrup.—*Courtesy of* Opera News, *by permission of the publisher, The Metropolitan Opera Guild, Inc.*

RIGHT: A rendition by the artist C. C. Curran of an 1895 production of Gounod's *Faust* at the Metropolitan. This opera, the first to be presented in the new opera house on October 22, 1883, had been performed 340 times at the close of the Metropolitan's seventy-fifth season (1959-1960).—*Courtesy of Metropolitan Opera Archives.*

PAGES

10-11 TOP LEFT: Christine Nilsson as Marguerite in *Faust.* The photograph shows the soprano as she appeared some years before she sang the role at the Metropolitan's opening night in 1883.—*From Culver Service.*

LOWER LEFT: Italo Campanini, Madame Nilsson's partner in the first Metropolitan *Faust.* Campanini also sang the roles of Raoul, Don José, Elvino, Don Ottavio, Edgardo, Boito's Faust, and Lohengrin in the 1883-1884 season. In this picture he has been identified as Manrico in *Il Trovatore,* but the costume may well be that of Raoul in *Les Huguenots.* —*From Culver Service.*

RIGHT: An 1883 restaurant scene entitled "After the Opera: From Amusement to Refection." The restaurant is possibly Delmonico's, a favorite after-the-opera spot of the eighties in New York City.—*From Culver Service.*

12-13 A fanciful composite delineation by Fred Morgan of personages from political and social life, as well as from journalism and the stage, as they might have appeared in the Metropolitan auditorium in 1891. The Baignoire boxes, which disappeared after the fire of 1892, are here visible beneath the Diamond Horseshoe. So is the old proscenium with its little doors for the use of artists in making their bows. The roster of celebrities assembled in the picture includes: 1. Cornelius Vanderbilt, capitalist; 2. Mary Anderson, actress; 3. Mrs. Samuel Colgate, social leader; 4. The Duchess of Marlborough, the American-born Lily Price whose wealth, acquired through her first husband, Louis Hamersley, helped restore Blenheim Castle. Four years later she became the stepmother-in-law of another American, the former Consuelo Vanderbilt; 5. Hugh J. Grant, Mayor of New York; 6. Mrs. Vanderbilt; 7. James Gordon Bennett, newspaper publisher; 8. Joseph Pulitzer, newspaper publisher; 9. Mrs. Herman Oelrichs, social leader; 10. Carl Schurz, U.S. Senator; 11. Charles A. Dana, newspaper editor; 12. William Dean Howells, novelist and noted editor; 13. George W. Childs, publisher, philanthropist; 14. Grover Cleveland, former President of the United States; 15. Jay Gould, railroad financier; 16. George W. Curtis, author, orator; 17. Mrs. Astor; 18. Unidentified; 19. Mrs. Cleveland; 20. Murat Halstead, author, journalist; 21. General Henry W. Slocum, U.S. Army, member of Congress; 22. Colonel Edward B. Fellows, underwriter, philanthropist; 23. Hamilton Fish, statesman; 24. Unidentified; 25. Edgar Saltus, society novelist and poet; 26. John Wanamaker, prominent merchant; 27. James G. Blaine, Secretary of State; 28. Thomas B. Reed, lawyer, parliamentarian; 29. Levi P. Morton, Vice President of the United States; 30. Mrs.

Cooper Hewitt, social leader; 31. Mrs. Potter Palmer, Chicago social leader; 32. Edmund Stanton, General Manager of the Metropolitan Opera; 33. F. Gray Griswold, sportsman, music connoisseur; 34. Chauncey M. Depew, lawyer, wit, U.S. Senator; 35. Benjamin Harrison, President of the United States; 36. Mrs. Middleton Burrill, Long Island hostess; 37. General T. W. Palmer, Minister to Spain; 38. Bret Harte, noted writer; 39. Andrew Carnegie, steel magnate; 40. Henry Villard, journalist, railroad promoter; 41. Mrs. Thomas M. Logan, wife of a great railroad magnate; 42. Mrs. S. Dillon Ripley, social leader; 43. Mrs. Adolph Ladenberg, society beauty and horsewoman; 44. William Henry Crane, actor; 45. Albert M. Palmer, theatrical manager; 46. John Jacob Astor, capitalist; 47. Ward McAllister, social leader; 48. D. Ogden Mills, railroad magnate and philanthropist; 49. Unidentified; 50. Edwin Booth, actor; 51. John Drew, actor; 52. Russell Sage, philanthropist; 53. Dan Frohman, theatrical manager; 54. Henry Clews, financier, author; 55. Joseph Jefferson, actor; 56. Collis P. Huntington, railroad magnate; 57. Augustin Daly, playwright, producer; 58. Lillian Russell, actress; 59. Mrs. Albert Stevens, social figure.—*From The Bettmann Archive.*

14-15 LEFT: Max Alvary created the role of the young Siegfried, in which he is here seen, in America and sang it from November 9, 1887, two years after his Metropolitan debut (as Don José in *Carmen*), until March 21, 1895. Critics of the day commended him for his "splendid vigor" in *Siegfried,* which they found "a strangely beautiful work."—*From Culver Service.*

RIGHT: Lilli Lehmann, who made her Metropolitan debut opposite Alvary (above) in *Carmen,* is seen here as Brünnhilde in *Die Walküre,* a role she assumed for the first time in her career five nights after her debut. "Her voice glorified the music," wrote Henry E. Krehbiel of the New York *Tribune,* and she continued to sing the role until December 28, 1898, later exchanging it for that of Sieglinde in the same opera.—*Courtesy of* Opera News, *by permission of the publisher, The Metropolitan Opera Guild, Inc.*

16-17 The original published version of this painting by J. Keppler, entitled "The War of the Operas," appeared in the American magazine *Puck* on February 11, 1891. The picture reflects the battle between the proponents of the Metropolitan's Wagnerian repertory, as conducted at the time by the long-haired, bespectacled Anton Seidl (*left center*), and the heroes and heroines of the Italian repertory, whose forces were led by Luigi Arditi (*right center*). The latter maestro had conducted operas in a supplementary season featuring the singers Patti and

Tamagno and presented at the Metropolitan by Henry Abbey in the spring of 1890. The success of this venture led to the official return of Abbey's Italian company in 1891-1892 at the conclusion of the German seasons.—*From The Bettmann Archive.*

18-19 Two views of the fire which burned out the Metropolitan auditorium and stage on August 27, 1892. In the large photograph at left may be seen the flooring which was laid over the orchestra seats when the opera house was used for charity balls. Missing from the small view of the Seventh Avenue façade are the two familiar roof stages which were installed in 1909 and 1921 under the management of Gatti-Casazza for additional rehearsal space.—*Courtesy of* Opera News, *by permission of the publisher, The Metropolitan Opera Guild, Inc.*

20-21 LEFT: This view, looking north on Broadway, shows the old Broadway Theater, which opened in 1888 with a production of Sardou's play *La Tosca.* The site had previously been occupied by the Metropolitan Concert Hall, an auditorium seating 800 which had been built in 1880. Here the first directors of the Metropolitan Opera House Company met before their own theater was completed. The photograph dates from the nineties.—*From The Bettmann Archive.*

RIGHT, *from top to bottom:* The first five general managers of the Metropolitan Opera House. Henry E. Abbey (1883-1884, the inaugural season) was known primarily as a speculator. He returned for the period 1891-1896. Leopold Damrosch (1884-1885) is remembered as a practical musician who helped to introduce Wagner to this country. Edmund Stanton (1885-1891), described as the most gentlemanly of impresarios, inherited the German company from Damrosch. Maurice Grau (1896-1903) brought together the greatest galaxy of stars ever heard at one time in the house. Heinrich Conried (1903-1908), practical man of the theater, introduced many new staging methods.—*Top and middle: Courtesy of* Opera News, *by permission of the publisher, The Metropolitan Opera Guild, Inc. Second and fourth: From Culver Service. Bottom: Courtesy of Metropolitan Opera Archives.*

22-23 This first flash photograph ever taken in the auditorium of the opera house was made by Ernest Marx on March 21, 1895, when the theater was occupied by a company headed by Walter Damrosch. The occasion was Max Alvary's hundredth performance in *Siegfried.* To obtain the photograph, fourteen ounces of an inflammable mixture were distributed over an iron frame placed at the edge of the stage, offering "thirty feet of lighting surface," according to a description in *Harper's Weekly.* The flash, ignited by an electric current of 350 amperes, lasted one forty-fifth of a second during the intermission preceding the second act.—*From Culver Service.*

24-25 Marcella Sembrich as Rosina, heroine of Rossini's *Barbiere di Siviglia.* This photograph was taken in 1898, fifteen years after the soprano's first appearance in the role during the inaugural season of the house. In the Lesson Scene, when the singer is permitted by tradition to insert her own choice of songs, Madame Sembrich used the Proch *Variations,* which she continued singing for many years. At her farewell in 1909, however, she inserted Johann Strauss's "Voices of Spring," an aria from *Sonnambula,* and "The Maiden's Wish" by Chopin.—*From Culver Service.*

26-27 FAR LEFT: Edouard de Reszke, the powerful Polish basso, as Méphistophélès in Gounod's *Faust,* a role which he sang with sardonic humor and majestic poise from February 1, 1892, six weeks after his Metropolitan debut as Frère Laurent in *Roméo et Juliette,* until April 27, 1903.—*Courtesy of* Opera News, *by permission of the publisher, The Metropolitan Opera Guild, Inc.*

LEFT CENTER: Jean de Reszke, elder brother of Edouard, started his career as a baritone, but rose to be the greatest tenor of his day. He is seen here as Tristan, which he sang at the Metropolitan from November 27, 1895, until his farewell on April 29, 1901.* His first appearances in New York were as Roméo, Raoul, Radames, and John of Leyden, and in the title role of *Lohengrin,* sung in an Italian version. But in ten years his repertory grew to include many heroic Wagnerian roles in the German language.—*Courtesy of* Opera News, *by permission of the publisher, The Metropolitan Opera Guild, Inc.*

TOP RIGHT: This photograph of Nellie Melba shows her as the heroine in Gounod's opera *Roméo et Juliette.* She first sang the part at the Metropolitan in January, 1894, sharing it that season with Emma Eames, and she was heard in the role nineteen times before her final appearance in the opera house as Violetta in a 1910 *Traviata.* The Australian soprano inscribed this photograph to a friend in 1913.—*Courtesy of* Opera News, *by permission of the publisher, The Metropolitan Opera Guild, Inc.*

*The performances ascribed to any singer in this volume refer only to appearances at the Metropolitan Opera House. These include appearances at gala concerts where single acts of various operas were sometimes presented.

PAGES

RIGHT CENTER: Lillian Nordica as Kundry in *Parsifal,* a role she first sang on Thanksgiving Day, 1904. The talents of this soprano from Farmington, Maine, won her the distinction of being the first American to be invited to sing at Bayreuth and the first Elsa in the history of the Bavarian Wagner festival.—*From Culver Service.*

FAR RIGHT: Emma Eames as Aida. Eames, like Nordica a product of the state of Maine, was trained in Europe and returned to make her first Metropolitan successes in French opera. In 1900, she sang her first New York Aida and continued in the part until 1909. She later maintained that she had learned the recipe for her make-up for the Ethiopian princess from a method used by Sarah Bernhardt in *Cléopâtre.* Her own additions to this process she would never divulge.—*From Culver Service.*

28-29 Metropolitan ballerinas rehearsing, probably in the 1890's, in the large salon on the Grand Tier of the opera house. The room was later taken over for use by Sherry's restaurant.—*Courtesy of The Museum of the City of New York.*

30-31 LEFT: Olive Fremstad as Salome, a role which the Swedish soprano sang only once at the Metropolitan. This was the ill-fated premiere of the Strauss music drama, based on Oscar Wilde's play, on January 22, 1907. The opera was immediately withdrawn at the request of the stockholders, not to be revived at the Metropolitan for twenty-seven years. —*From Culver Service.*

LOWER CENTER: This cartoon by W. A. Rogers, entitled "Discharged Without Honor," shows Father Knickerbocker indignantly banishing the lascivious heroine of *Salome* from the city.—*From The Bettmann Archive.*

RIGHT: Emma Calvé is seen as Carmen, the fascinating heroine of Bizet's melodrama. For ten years (December, 1893, to March, 1904) Calvé *was* Carmen to the American public and Carmen, Calvé, although the soprano's interpretation changed through a decade's experience, becoming more abandoned and improvisational.—*From Culver Service.*

32-33 Opening-night view of the Metropolitan in 1906, with Geraldine Farrar making her debut as Juliette in Gounod's lyric version of the Shakespeare play. The new proscenium which is shown here was designed by Carrère and Hastings and installed in 1903, while the new curtains were hung in 1905. Though this "photograph" is actually a composite of two views—the one of the stage set, the other of the audience—it has long been accepted as a legitimate depiction because of its essential authenticity.—*From Culver Service.*

34-35 LEFT: Enrico Caruso as Canio in *Pagliacci.* It is for this role that the Metropolitan's great tenor will, perhaps, be longest remembered. He sang it eighty-one times in the house from December 9, 1903, a fortnight after his debut in *Rigoletto,* to December 8, 1920, when he was stricken with acute pain during the performance, necessitating a delay of twenty minutes. He died the following August.—*Courtesy of* Opera News, *by permission of the publisher, The Metropolitan Opera Guild, Inc.*

LOWER RIGHT: Cartoons by Caruso. From top to bottom: a caricature of his impresario, Gatti-Casazza, shown here with a handful of stars in his coat pocket; the tenor and Geraldine Farrar, whose costume suggests Madame Butterfly; and the impeccable conductor Arturo Toscanini.—*Courtesy of Marziale Sisca, publisher of* Caricatures by Enrico Caruso *(New York: 1951).*

36-37 This historic scene was photographed on the Metropolitan stage during a rehearsal for the world premiere of Umberto Giordano's *Madame Sans Gêne.* This opera, based on Sardou's play of Napoleon's career, received fourteen performances from 1915 to 1918. Geraldine Farrar was featured in the vivacious title role. In the picture, Toscanini, who conducted the work during the first season only, stands at the left. Gatti-Casazza sits at the center. Shortly after the sixth performance of the new work, Toscanini retired permanently from the Metropolitan.— *From Culver Service.*

38-39 The Triumphal Scene from *Aida* (Act II, Scene 2) as it appeared on November 16, 1908, the opening night of Gatti-Casazza's first season as general manager at the Metropolitan. At the front of the stage, left to right, stand the principals: Antonio Scotti (arm akimbo) as Amonasro, Emmy Destinn as Aida, Caruso (in profile) as Radames, Giulio Rossi as the King, Louise Homer as Amneris, and Adamo Didur (outstretched arm) as Ramfis. The then new production was created by Sala and Paravicini of Milan. Arturo Toscanini was the conductor.—*Courtesy of Metropolitan Opera Archives.*

40-41 Claudia Muzio in the role of Tosca, which she sang at the Metropolitan from her debut on December 4, 1916, opposite Caruso and Scotti, until April 22, 1921, sharing the role with Farrar. It then fell to Maria Jeritza. Muzio was last heard at the opera house on January 10, 1934, as Santuzza in *Cavalleria Rusticana.*—*Courtesy of* Opera News, *by permission of the publisher, The Metropolitan Opera Guild, Inc.*

42-43 FAR LEFT: Antonio Scotti, whose career extended over thirty-four uninterrupted seasons at the Metropolitan, is seen here as Falstaff in Verdi's opera by the same name. The baritone sang this role from 1909 to 1927 and gained an immediate artistic triumph in his first impersonation of the "fat knight." —*Courtesy of* Opera News, *by permission of the publisher, The Metropolitan Opera Guild, Inc.*

TOP, LEFT CENTER: Frieda Hempel introduced the *Rosenkavalier* Marschallin to this country on December 9, 1913, and continued in the role until 1917, two years before her retirement from the Metropolitan.—*From Culver Service.*

LEFT CENTER: Emmy Destinn's Aida was featured in the premiere performance of Gatti's regime in 1908 and endured for thirteen years, being famed for the soprano's great power and dramatic gifts.— *Courtesy of* Opera News, *by permission of the publisher, The Metropolitan Opera Guild, Inc.*

BOTTOM, LEFT CENTER: Alma Gluck, seen here as Mimi in *La Bohème,* sang at the Metropolitan for three seasons only, appearing in the last of five such performances on March 20, 1912. Her final Metropolitan performance was as the Happy Shade in Gluck's *Orfeo* a fortnight later, though she subsequently took part in Sunday-night concerts in the house.—*From Culver Service.*

TOP, RIGHT CENTER: Though he did not create the role of Boris Godunov at the Metropolitan, Feodor Chaliapin seemed indispensable in the cast of Mussorgsky's opera from December 9, 1921, until March 14, 1929, singing the part in his native Russian and demonstrating the utmost nobility of vocal and dramatic art.—*Courtesy of* Opera News, *by permission of the publisher, The Metropolitan Opera Guild, Inc.*

BOTTOM, RIGHT CENTER: Luisa Tetrazzini appeared at the Metropolitan during the season of 1911-1912, singing Violetta, Gilda, and Lucia (as seen here), when her brilliant coloratura passages excited the public to heated enthusiasm.—*From Culver Service.*

FAR RIGHT: Lucrezia Bori's Juliette brought the essence of romantic youth and delicacy to the Metropolitan for ten seasons, giving rise to unfounded but sympathetic rumors of a romance with the most glamorous of her Roméos, Edward Johnson.—*Courtesy of* Opera News, *by permission of the publisher, The Metropolitan Opera Guild, Inc.*

44-45 LEFT: The seduction scene in the second act of *Parsifal* is enacted here by Orville Harrold and Margarete Matzenauer. The opera was sung at the Metropolitan by these artists for two seasons in an English version written by the New York *Tribune* music critic, Henry E. Krehbiel. Their first performance together was on February 19, 1920, the first attempt to present Wagner in English at the Metropolitan. *Parsifal,* in a new setting by Joseph Urban, was the first German opera to be revived after World War I.—*Courtesy of Metropolitan Opera Archives.*

RIGHT: Frances Alda and Leo Slezak sang *Otello* at the Metropolitan from the tenor's debut performance on November 17, 1909, to January 31, 1913, reaching a total of thirteen performances together. "The audience fairly gasped when Herr Slezak made his entrance," noted Mr. Krehbiel, critic of the New York *Tribune,* who found the tenor "superb in his . . . brokenhearted despair" in the last act (shown here).—*Courtesy of Metropolitan Opera Archives.*

46-47 TOP, FAR LEFT: When Amelita Galli-Curci made her Metropolitan debut on November 14, 1921, as Violetta in *La Traviata* (the role depicted here), her voice was hailed as "one of the most beautiful the public has heard." Chosen to open the first season after the death of Caruso, the soprano met the ordeal with traces of nervousness, though supported by a strong cast and favored with new settings and costumes. Her "plaintive tenderness" was recorded by William J. Henderson, critic of the New York *Sun.* She continued in the part for eight seasons.— *Courtesy of* Opera News, *by permission of the publisher, The Metropolitan Opera Guild, Inc.*

TOP, LEFT CENTER: The career of Louise Homer endured for thirty years at the Metropolitan. Her most famous parts were the title role in Gluck's *Orfeo,* Laura in *La Gioconda,* Dalila, and Mona, heroine of Horatio Parker's prize work by the same name. She was also noted for her interpretation of Azucena in *Il Trovatore,* Waltraute in *Götterdämmerung,* and Amneris, as she is shown here, in *Aida.* It was in this last role that she made her debut on December 22, 1900, and she continued singing it until December 14, 1927.—*Courtesy of* Opera News, *by permission of the publisher, The Metropolitan Opera Guild, Inc.*

TOP, LEFT CENTER: Beniamino Gigli, one of the tenors to inherit the mantle of Caruso at the opera house, is seen here as Vasco da Gama, the hero of Meyerbeer's *l'Africana,* which he sang from March 21, 1923, to March 19, 1932. "The brilliance and effect of Meyerbeer's music were congenial to Gigli," reports the music historian Irving Kolodin.—*Courtesy of Metropolitan Opera Archives.*

LOWER LEFT: Rosa Ponselle interpreted the sinister Margared in *Le Roi d'Ys* during the season 1921-1922, when she sang it on four occasions. Only the familiar Aubade from this opera seems to have survived in public performance, since the work was speedily withdrawn, in spite of one of the most baleful operatic delineations ever recorded by the camera.—*Courtesy of* Opera News, *by permission of the publisher, The Metropolitan Opera Guild, Inc.*

TOP RIGHT: Maria Jeritza sang her first Metropolitan Elisabeth in *Tannhäuser* on February 1, 1923, when the opera was revived for the first time since World

War I. She continued in the role for nine seasons, singing it on twenty-nine occasions.—*Courtesy of* Opera News, *by permission of the publisher, The Metropolitan Opera Guild, Inc.*

RIGHT CENTER: Lotte Lehmann was unforgettably identified with the *Rosenkavalier* Marschallin in the decade of her Metropolitan performances from January 4, 1935, when she first assumed the role in New York. In the previous season she had made her debut as Sieglinde.—*Courtesy of* Opera News, *by permission of the publisher, The Metropolitan Opera Guild, Inc.*

FAR RIGHT: Giuseppe DeLuca made his Metropolitan debut as Figaro in Rossini's *Il Barbiere di Siviglia* on November 25, 1915, and sang it off and on for twenty years, together with fifty-one other important baritone parts. He returned in 1940 at the age of sixty-four for his forty-third impersonation of the ebullient barber, completing 702 Metropolitan performances before his farewell at the age of seventy. —*Courtesy of* Opera News, *by permission of the publisher, The Metropolitan Opera Guild, Inc.*

48-49 Edward Johnson is shown here as Peter Ibbetson, the title role in Deems Taylor's opera. The work endured through four seasons, a record up to this time for any American opera, and enlisted Lucrezia Bori, Edward Johnson, and Lawrence Tibbett as principals for all sixteen performances. In 1935, Johnson became general manager of the opera company, replacing Herbert Witherspoon, who had died a few weeks after his appointment to the office. —*Courtesy of Metropolitan Opera Archives.*

50-51 The third-act wedding scene in Edward Johnson's new production of Mozart's *Nozze di Figaro,* designed by Jonel Jorgulesco, staged by Herbert Graf, and first presented on February 20, 1940. The Johnson revival ushered in a period of fresh popularity for Mozart, enhanced by a cast led by Elisabeth Rethberg, Ezio Pinza, John Brownlee, Bidu Sayao, and Risë Stevens, under the baton of Ettore Panizza. —*Photo by Louis Melançon.*

52-53 FAR LEFT: Ezio Pinza as Don Giovanni. It was Pinza's magnetic and buoyantly-voiced interpretation which was largely credited with the success of Mozart's opera as revived on November 29, 1929. The event also presaged the bass-baritone's success as Figaro a decade later, but Pinza continued to sing Don Giovanni until his final Metropolitan season, which he opened in this same part in a special pre-season gala on November 7, 1947.—*Courtesy of* Opera News, *by permission of the publisher, The Metropolitan Opera Guild, Inc.*

FAR RIGHT: Helen Traubel sang her first *Walküre* Brünnhilde on December 6, 1941, two years after her Wagnerian debut as Sieglinde in the same work and nearly five after her first appearance at the Metropolitan as Mary Rutledge, in Walter Damrosch's *Man Without a Country.*—*Courtesy of* Opera News, *by permission of the publisher, The Metropolitan Opera Guild, Inc.*

LOWER LEFT CENTER: Lily Pons sang Marie, heroine of *La Fille du Régiment,* on nine occasions when Donizetti's comedy was revived for her in 1940 after a lapse of twenty-two years. The press commended her vivacity and virtuosity, and she was chosen to open the 1942-1943 season in the role.—*From Culver Service.*

LOWER CENTER: Giovanni Martinelli sang his first Metropolitan Otello on December 22, 1937, in his twenty-fifth season with the company. Despite the fact that the tenor was then past fifty, he was praised by the critic of the New York *Sun,* among others, for bringing "fervor and comprehension" to the music in this climax to a notable career.— *Courtesy of* Opera News, *by permission of the publisher, The Metropolitan Opera Guild, Inc.*

TOP RIGHT: Lawrence Tibbett enacted the vengeful husband, Michele, in Puccini's melodrama *Il Tabarro* when the work was revived at the Metropolitan on January 5, 1946, twenty-seven years after its world premiere on the same stage. This was the baritone's twenty-third season with the company.—*Courtesy of Metropolitan Opera Archives.*

BOTTOM RIGHT: Grace Moore had already appeared in a film version of Charpentier's opera *Louise* when she first sang the title role of that work at the Metropolitan in its revival performance of January 28, 1939. This photograph shows her as she appeared in the film, which was supervised by the composer himself.—*Courtesy of Metropolitan Opera Archives.*

54-55 LEFT: Kirsten Flagstad sang her first Metropolitan Isolde on February 6, 1935, four days after her eloquent debut as Sieglinde. She soon became the most famous of all Wagnerian sopranos, singing Isolde opposite Lauritz Melchior's Tristan (shown with her here) on forty-nine occasions until her farewell in the role on April 12, 1941. The Danish tenor was no longer with the company when Madame Flagstad returned for a glorious reappearance as Isolde on January 22, 1951.—*Courtesy of* Opera News, *by permission of the publisher, The Metropolitan Opera Guild, Inc.*

RIGHT: In this painting the noted artist Reginald Marsh satirized the opera audience of 1936—a time when the Depression had made society's old regime a target for levity. Two rows of boxes were still to be seen at the opera house at this time. The upper tier, known as the Grand Tier boxes, was removed during the summer of 1940, after the house was purchased by the Metropolitan Opera Association from the stockholders, leaving the Diamond Horseshoe on the Parterre level as the only remaining boxes, thirty-five in number, from the original 122 boxes of 1883.—*Painting by Reginald Marsh, courtesy of University of Arizona Art Gallery.*

56-57 These photographs were taken at a meeting of The Metropolitan Opera Guild held at the opera house on October 22, 1958, to celebrate the seventy-fifth anniversary of the founding of the theater. On this occasion (*left*), a portrait by the British painter Simon Elwes was presented to Mrs. August Belmont, the Guild's Founder and President Emeritus. Standing with Mrs. Belmont (*left to right*) are: Langdon Van Norden, President of the Opera Guild; Anthony A. Bliss, President of the Metropolitan Opera Association; and Lauder Greenway, Chairman of the Metropolitan Opera Board of Directors. The seventy-fifth anniversary audience was shown portraits of the Metropolitan's greatest singers, projected on a screen. The photograph at right depicts the screening of a portrait of Caruso. The Metropolitan's assistant manager, Francis Robinson (small illuminated figure), was one of five commentators on this occasion.—*Photos by Gjon Mili.*

58-59 Rudolf Bing, who assumed the management of the Metropolitan in 1950, is shown here beside the heroic marble bust of a predecessor, the late Giulio Gatti-Casazza, who reigned from 1908 to 1935. The statue is the work of the late Frederick MacMonnies. —*Photo by Gjon Mili.*

60-61 Posters beside the brightly lighted marquee of the Metropolitan Opera House announce the season's repertory and casts.—*Photo by Gjon Mili.*

62-63 The Metropolitan box office. Photographs of the entire current Metropolitan roster always line the walls of the Broadway lobby and are changed each year. They are arranged in haphazard order, since the Metropolitan officially recognizes no stars. The two most clearly visible next to the window where Harvey Jensen sells tickets are Victoria de los Angeles and Antonietta Stella.—*Photos by Gjon Mili.*

64-65 LEFT: Standees crowd the space at the rear of the orchestra seats just before the beginning of a performance.—*Photo by Gjon Mili.*
RIGHT: A Parterre box is still considered a highly desirable location for opening-night performances, benefits, galas, and certain subscription performances.—*Photo by Gjon Mili.*

66-67 Thomas Schippers, conducting *Lohengrin* at the Metropolitan on February 11, 1959. Schippers' first appearance at the opera house was as the conductor of Donizetti's *Don Pasquale* and a ballet entitled *Soirée,* arranged by Benjamin Britten from Rossini music, on December 23, 1955, when he was barely twenty-five years old. In the next four seasons, he added *La Bohème, Les Contes d'Hoffmann, Carmen, Un Ballo in Maschera, Der fliegende Holländer,* and *La Forza del Destino* to his Metropolitan repertory.—*Photo by Gjon Mili.*

68-69 In this scene from the third act of Verdi's *Aida,* Gloria Davy, singing the title role on January 3, 1959, crouches at the feet of Robert Merrill, as Aida's father, the Ethiopian King Amonasro. *Aida* is by far the most frequently performed opera on the Metropolitan stage, having had 441 performances during the first seventy-five years of the history of the house.—*Photo by Gjon Mili.*

70-71 The Triumphal Scene from *Aida* (Act II, Scene 2) as seen from the fly bridge at the north of the stage. In this photograph, the ballet concludes its dance before the King, who shares the throne at the right with the High Priest, Ramfis.—*Photo by Gjon Mili.*

72-73 Scenery for a production of *Aida* is here stacked against the west (Seventh Avenue) wall of the opera house. Some of it is being loaded into trucks so that it may be taken to the warehouse, where it will await the next performance of the same opera.— *Photo by Gjon Mili.*

74-75 In this photograph, the Metropolitan stage is set for the first scene of *Aida* (*extreme left*). Scenery for later acts stands at the right. The royal throne may be seen at lower left center, the ceremonial fans at top center. A stagehand rests (*top center*), awaiting the rise of the curtain. This production of *Aida* was designed by Rolf Gérard and was first staged on the opening night of the 1951-1952 season.—*Photo by Gjon Mili.*

76-77 Dimitri Mitropoulos conducted *Tosca, Boris Godunov, Cavalleria Rusticana, Pagliacci, Eugene Onegin,* and *Vanessa* during the 1958-1959 season, when this photograph was taken.—*Photo by Gjon Mili.*

78-79 The renowned Broadway director José Quintero came to the Metropolitan at the invitation of Rudolf Bing to direct the new productions of *Cavalleria Rusticana* and *Pagliacci,* first seen on November 7, 1958. In this photograph, Quintero instructs the chorus, assisted by Executive Stage Manager Michael Manuel (*left center*).—*Photo by Gjon Mili.*

PAGES

80-81 LEFT: Stage director Herbert Graf instructs Cesare Siepi in details of fencing, preparatory to the basso's performances as Don Giovanni.

RIGHT: A stage rehearsal of Verdi's *Macbeth* in January, 1959, shows Leonard Warren and Leonie Rysanek in the leading roles (*right center*). Assisting at rehearsal (*left to right*): Victor Trucco, Martin Rich, Carl Ebert (standing), Otello Ceroni, Etienne Barone, Stanley Levine, Patrick Tavernia, and Calvin Marsh.—*Photos by Gjon Mili.*

82-83 Carl Ebert, the distinguished artistic director of the Städtische Oper in Berlin and co-founder of the Glyndebourne Festival, is here seen during a rehearsal of Verdi's *Macbeth,* which he came to New York to direct at the invitation of the general manager for the Metropolitan premiere of the work on February 5, 1959.—*Photo by Gjon Mili.*

84-85 LEFT: The famous Russian ballerina Alexandra Danilova demonstrates her choreography for the ballet *Les Diamants,* in preparation for the special ballet evening which was presented on March 22, 1959. At her left stand John Gutman, assistant manager, and Mattlyn Gavers, the Metropolitan's ballet mistress.—*Photo by Gjon Mili.*

RIGHT: Antony Tudor, Director of the Metropolitan Ballet and the Ballet School, explains to his pupils his belief that the dance, like all art forms, must originate in the brain.—*Photo by Gjon Mili.*

86-87 A young ballerina starts her daily half-hour practice at the bar in the Metropolitan's Fortieth Street roof stage.—*Photo by Gjon Mili.*

88-89 Lupe Serrano, prima ballerina of the 1958-1959 ballet, heads her fellow dancers in *Les Diamants,* a new ballet to the music of Bériot with choreography by Danilova. The dance was presented under Walter Taussig's baton during the special ballet program of March 22, 1959.—*Photo by Gjon Mili.*

90-91 Property man Irving Stein arranges the masks used as background for the witches' scene in the 1959 Metropolitan production of Verdi's *Macbeth,* fastening them on a frame to hang above the stage.—*Photo by Gjon Mili.*

92-93 LEFT: Members of the scenic department on the paint bridge, thirty feet above stage, execute a border for the 1959 production of Johann Strauss's *Gypsy Baron.* The sets were designed by Rolf Gérard.—*Photo by Gjon Mili.*

RIGHT: Young members of the ballet remove their make-up after a rehearsal of Ponchielli's *La Gioconda.*—*Photo by Gjon Mili.*

94-95 LEFT: Costumes hang from waistband tapes outside the Metropolitan wardrobes. Below them stand the hampers which will be packed for the spring tour.—*Photo by Gjon Mili.*

RIGHT: Angelo Casamassa, dresser for the male artists, helps the basso Cesare Siepi, bewigged and already made up, into his costume as Don Giovanni. Siepi, who came to the Metropolitan in 1950 to sing King Philip II in the opening-night *Don Carlo,* also sang Méphistophélès in Gounod's *Faust* during his first season and was assigned to *Don Giovanni* for the first time on November 26, 1952.—*Photo by Gjon Mili.*

96-97 Tenor Kurt Baum preens in front of a backstage mirror before his appearance as the Drum Major in Alban Berg's *Wozzeck,* an atonal music drama introduced into the Metropolitan repertory on March 5, 1959.—*Photos by Gjon Mili.*

98-99 Alice Plotkin examines her make-up for the role of the child in *Wozzeck.*—*Photo by Gjon Mili.*

100-101 LEFT: As the curtain is about to rise, Executive Stage Manager Michael Manuel signals for silence. —*Photo by Gjon Mili.*

RIGHT: Prompter Otello Ceroni is shown as he appears from the lower steps of the ladder which leads to his narrow seat at stage front center. Strong lights burn under his metal hood so that his gestures can be seen easily by the singers onstage.—*Photo by Gjon Mili.*

102-103 LEFT: Erich Leinsdorf conducts the Metropolitan orchestra. The fence behind his podium is painted white in order that he may be more readily seen by the singers.—*Photo by Gjon Mili.*

RIGHT: Erich Leinsdorf's baton vibrates in his right hand as he signals with his left hand for diminished volume.—*Photo by Gjon Mili.*

104-105 Leonard Warren, the great American baritone, had risen to the summit of his career before his untimely death on stage in a performance of *La Forza del Destino* on March 4, 1960. He had sung 410 performances in a total of twenty-six parts, among them such title roles as Rigoletto, Falstaff, Macbeth, and Simon Boccanegra. He is here shown as Tonio, the deformed clown of *Pagliacci,* who makes his second-act entrance playing a big bass drum to announce that the evening show is about to start.—*Photo by Gjon Mili.*

106-107 Mario Del Monaco as Canio in *Pagliacci* sings *Vesti la giubba* ("On with the motley [a clown's tunic]") at the close of the first act.—*Photo by Gjon Mili.*

108-109 Zinka Milanov as Santuzza joins the Sicilian peasants in *Cavalleria Rusticana,* singing the Easter Hymn, *Inneggiamo, il Signor non e morto* ("Let us sing, the Lord is not dead").—*Photo by Gjon Mili.*

110-111 In this photograph Risë Stevens as Carmen is seen attempting to resist the brigadier Don José (Richard Tucker), who has been ordered to arrest her for brawling with another worker in the cigarette factory. After the guards have cleared the street, Carmen will sing the *Seguidilla* and tease Don José into letting her escape. This realistic production, designed by Rolf Gérard and staged by Tyrone Guthrie, was first presented at the Metropolitan on January 31, 1952, when Mr. Tucker was heard as Don José for the first time. Miss Stevens had sung the role of Carmen at the opera house since December 28, 1945, but she placed a new emphasis on the fatalism of Bizet's heroine under Mr. Guthrie's direction.—*Photo by Gjon Mili.*

112-113 LEFT: Antonietta Stella as Cio-Cio-San in *Madama Butterfly* joins Suzuki (*not shown*) in the Flower Duet—*Gettiamo a mani piene* ("Let us scatter handfuls")—near the close of the second act of Puccini's opera. Stella was trained in authentic Japanese posture by Yoshio Aoyama. Her costumes were designed by Ming Cho Lee.—*Photo by Gjon Mili.*
RIGHT: Antonietta Stella as Cio-Cio-San (standing) with Margaret Roggero as her maid Suzuki at the opening of the third act of *Madama Butterfly* in the 1958 production designed by Motohiro Nagasaka.—*Photo by Gjon Mili.*

114-115 In Mozart's *Così fan tutte,* Act II, Scene 3, the cynical Don Alfonso (standing, *left center*), played (December 17, 1955) by Lorenzo Alvary, urges the ladies Fiordiligi and Dorabella (left to right, Eleanor Steber and Blanche Thebom), further encouraged by their maid Despina (Patrice Munsel, seated on the ground) to accept the addresses of their suitors, Ferrando and Guglielmo (left to right, Cesare Valletti and Frank Guarrera), who have appeared disguised as Albanian noblemen in the ladies' garden. —*Photo by Gjon Mili.*

116-117 LEFT: Elisabeth Soederstroem as Susanna in *Le Nozze di Figaro,* Act IV.—*Photo by Gjon Mili.*
RIGHT: Licia Albanese as Violetta in *La Traviata,* Act I. Her ball gown of white lace flounces was designed by Karinska. She is singing *Sempre libera* ("Always free").—*Photo by Gjon Mili.*

118-119 Maria Meneghini Callas as Violetta in *La Traviata,* Act I. She is singing the *Brindisi,* a toast to pleasure. —*Photo by Louis Melançon.*

120-121 Birgit Nilsson as Isolde, the role of her Metropolitan debut on December 18, 1959. The Swedish soprano was hailed on the front pages of the New York press the following day as "a true princess, not only in Ireland but in all the world of opera the possessor of a magnificent voice . . of extraordinary brightness." She is here seen in the first act of Wagner's *Tristan und Isolde,* crying to the winds and waves to wreck the ship which is taking her to Cornwall against her will.—*Photo by Gjon Mili.*

122-123 Otto Edelmann as Hans Sachs, leading figure of Wagner's *Die Meistersinger von Nürnberg,* is seen from behind the hat of a fellow citizen. He is hailed by apprentices and mastersingers (*at extreme right*). Among the latter are: Osie Hawkins, Louis Sgarro. and Ezio Flagello.—*Photo by Gjon Mili.*

124-125 LEFT: Karl Liebl, as Lohengrin, shown at his first entrance as a dream figure.—*Photo by Gjon Mili.*
RIGHT: Aase Nordmo Loevberg as Elsa in Act I of Wagner's mystical opera, singing *Du trugest zu ihm meine Klage* ("Thou gavest him my supplication"). —*Photo by Gjon Mili.*

126-127 Jerome Hines in the title role of Mussorgsky's *Boris Godunov,* Act IV, Scene 2. At center, Charles Kullman as Prince Shuisky; at right, Calvin Marsh as Shchelkalov, Secretary of the Duma.—*Photo by Gjon Mili.*

128-129 Cesare Siepi as Don Giovanni in the Mozart opera, Act II, Scene 5.—*Photo by Gjon Mili.*

130-131 LEFT: George London as Baron Scarpia in Puccini's *Tosca,* Act I.—*Photo by Gjon Mili.*
RIGHT: Renata Tebaldi as Tosca at the finale of Puccini's melodrama. This was the opening-night performance of the 1958-1959 season. The photograph shows Mario Del Monaco as Cavaradossi, lying dead on the battlements of the Castel Sant' Angelo. Overhead the statue of the archangel Michael sheathes its sword in memory of a plague from which the city of Rome was long ago saved. The action is symbolic of the fact that Scarpia, the opera's villain, is also dead.—*Photo by Gjon Mili.*

132-133 The crowd in the Grand Tier foyer at one of the intermissions on opening night, October 27, 1958. Sherry's bar and restaurant lie beyond the arch.— *Photo by Gjon Mili.*

134-135 LEFT: Chorus members Dina De Salvo (*left*) and Pearl Goldsmith (*right*) hurry to their dressing rooms during the intermission of *Don Giovanni.*— *Photo by Gjon Mili.*

PAGES

RIGHT: Young ballerinas pause at the water cooler after their appearance in the first-act carnival scene from Amilcare Ponchielli's *La Gioconda.—Photo by Gjon Mili.*

136-137 Three young New Yorkers, Wendy Watts, Margay Ferguson, and Rita Cannon, watch an opera from a Parterre box.—*Photo by Gjon Mili.*

138-139 A maid sits guard by the Parterre boxes at the end of intermission, while two members of the audience chat in the lobby beyond.—*Photos by Gjon Mili.*

140-141 Stage director Carl Ebert raps the wooden floor of the stage for good luck before the curtain rises on the Metropolitan premiere of Verdi's *Macbeth,* which he staged.—*Photo by Gjon Mili.*

142-143 Leonie Rysanek in the sleepwalking scene of *Macbeth* (Act IV, Scene 2). The Metropolitan's first production of this work, presented on February 5, 1959, was designed by Caspar Neher.—*Photos by Gjon Mili.*

144-145 Eleanor Steber as Vanessa in Act I of Samuel Barber's opera of the same name, with a libretto by Gian-Carlo Menotti. The opera was first seen January 15, 1958. Costumes and settings were designed by Cecil Beaton.—*Photo by Gjon Mili.*

146-147 LEFT: A group of the children from the last scene of the 1959 production of *Wozzeck.—Photo by Gjon Mili.*
RIGHT: Hermann Uhde as Wozzeck on the evening of March 5, 1959. At left, the sadistic doctor, Karl Doench; at right, the maniacal captain, Paul Franke. —*Photo by Gjon Mili.*

148-149 Karl Doench, the doctor in *Wozzeck,* takes his curtain call.—*Photo by Gjon Mili.*

150-151 Nell Rankin, as Ortrud in *Lohengrin,* acknowledges her applause after the performance of February 11, 1959.—*Photo by Gjon Mili.*

152-153 Giulietta Simionato, still in the make-up of her sensational debut as the ancient gypsy Azucena in Verdi's *Trovatore,* smiles at her reception on October 26, 1959.—*Photo by Gjon Mili.*

154-155 LEFT: This dressing room, known as Number 15, was occupied by Geraldine Farrar during her career at the Metropolitan. It is the only one in the history of the house to have been reserved for the exclusive use of one star. Today, like all other dressing rooms, it is shared by various artists.—*Photo by Gjon Mili.*
RIGHT: Scuffed slippers lie on the floor of the ballet dressing room, a reminder of the turmoil of preparation for a performance.—*Photo by Gjon Mili.*

156-157 This photograph of the Metropolitan Opera House shows the building as it appears after midnight from its southeast corner, with the Broadway marquee at the extreme right. Surrounding it in its last years are the skyscrapers of the wholesale-clothing district which have replaced the banks, churches, and theaters of an earlier era.—*Photo by Gjon Mili.*

158-159 A silver bust of Enrico Caruso, made by Cifariello in Bellosguardo, Florence, about 1908, was presented by the tenor's widow to the Metropolitan on October 29, 1947. It stands near an exit of the Family Circle, where the tenor would have recognized many friends among the opera-lovers who still prefer this location.—*Photo by Gjon Mili.*

Index

---

*The numbers thus indicated refer to pages on which pictures of the subject matter appear.